Hunting Season

Insights for Living
from a Seasoned Hunter

By Maury De Young

Foreward by Mark Romanack

Artwork by Bruce R. Witt

Scripture taken from the HOLY BIBLE, NEW INTERNATIONAL VERSION ® NIV ®. Copyright © 1973, 1978, 1984 by International Bible Society. Used by permission of Zondervan. All rights reserved.

Library of Congress Control Number: 2002095338

ISBN 0-9725539 – 0 - 8

First Printing, December 2002

Additional copies of this book are available by mail.

Maury De Young
610-52nd St SE
Kentwood, MI 49548
616-534-0085
mdeyoung@kcrc.org

Printed in the U. S. A. by
Morris Publishing
3212 East Highway 30
Kearney, NE 68847
1-800-650-7888

CONTENTS

To God who gave us this marvelous world for us to enjoy and especially for the fantastic gift of his Son, Jesus Christ, who has given me real reason for living.

To my wonderful wife, Cheryl.

To my children: Chris, Michelle, Lisa, and Tim.

To the newest members of our family: Arlene, Gene, and Tom.

To the youngest little "hunter" in our family, our first new grandchild, Lucas Michael.

And in memory of our youngest son, Derrick, who at age 16 was taken home to Jesus on November 23, 2002, as a result of an automobile accident. Memories of him stream through this entire book.

FORWARD

By Mark Romanack

They say that everyone has a calling, a reason for being or a greater purpose in life. For most of us identifying this calling is a fleeting experience that we somehow never connect with. Life leads us down many paths and often our dreams and desires get put on hold in favor of responsibility or other daily issues.

Maury De Young has been blessed with not one, but two callings. A graduate of Calvin Theological Seminary and a practicing pastor since 1974, Pastor Maury has shared his love of God and Christianity with countless individuals from all walks of life. His penetrating sermons are one of his greatest shared gifts. I can say from personal experience that Pastor Maury's weekly sermons have an uncanny ability to get inside a person's head. Somehow his message always feels as if it was written especially for my family and me.

Maury shares his remarkable communication skills with the members of his church every day, but church members are not the only folks who benefit. In the fall of 1991 Maury started an outreach group aimed at men, women and children who enjoy hunting, fishing and the outdoor sports. An avid sportsman himself, Maury recognized that by combining his love of God and love of the outdoors he could better reach both the members of his church and countless seekers in the community who have not cemented a relationship with God.

From modest beginnings that involved just 35 individuals, the Kelloggsville Church Sportspersons Club has connected with over 8,000 people. Monthly seminars that attract hundreds of outdoor minded people are the focus of the KCSC, but many other activities including wild game dinners, fly tying classes, sport show appearances, archery shoots, big buck contests and a Kid's Trails program have all developed as part of this amazingly successful outreach group.

Maury has also shared what he has learned with many other churches. Similar outreach programs are now popping up all over the country thanks to the vision, support and guidance of Maury De Young.

Maury De Young is a gifted man who has found a wonderful way to share his love of God and love of the outdoors with all who will listen. Each outreach program is ended with a brief devotional. The programs offered aren't intended to pressure folks into accepting Christianity, but rather to provide those who want more from a Christian relationship a place to start.

This book is an extension of Maury's tireless work and devotion. Read on and let Maury lift your spirits and open your horizons.

ACKNOWLEDGEMENTS

This book is the result of the prayers, encouragement, and support of many people. I am not able to mention every person has helped with this project. I will specifically highlight a few that have gone far beyond any call of duty or responsibility.

Thank you to my family. I want to begin by thanking my wife, Cheryl, who has provided tremendous support for me in my ministry and who has been a wonderful mother. She has also allowed me to spend time in the out of doors with my children. Each of my children have encouraged me and helped me in this project. As you have seen, my family members have often been involved in these stories. I treasure those memories of the times we have spent together in hunting.

A very special thanks to my daughter, Michelle, who worked fervently, enthusiastically, and intensely to complete the layout for this book. My other daughter, Lisa, deserves recognition as my Administrative Assistant for some of our Sportsperson's Club activities.

Mark and Mari Romanack have become wonderful friends, but they also have been great coaches in this process. I do not know if I would have continued with this book without your guidance, direction, and encouragement.

My sister-in-law, Carol Christians, performed the initial editing. Her sensitive suggestions guided me to improve what I was doing.

Kelloggsville Church Sportsperson's Club Board and Leaders have been an excellent team to work with. I am amazed at what God has done in and through our club. You, as leaders, are to be commended for your involvement. Thank you for the support you have given to make this book possible.

Paul Vander Molen has been my staff support person. You have become a close friend and I can't begin to thank you for the support, encouragement, and challenges that you have given me in my work and in this venture.

Bruce R. Witt, although our reduced size doesn't do justice to the beauty of your original drawings, I want to thank you for your contribution to complete this project.

Thank you to Kelloggsville Church staff who has given suggestions, help, and support to finish this book. Special thanks and recognition needs to be given to our church secretary, Mary Lou Hofman, and to our Director of Ministries, Jacque Bolt who have advised me and given me suggestions along they way.

Thanks to Kelloggsville Church board who allowed me to take some sabbatical time, which included some time to work on this book.

I also want to thank Gerald Bergstom and the staff at Morris Publishing for guiding me through this process and for giving helping advice for my first book.

INTRODUCTION

Fall is my favorite time of the year. I like the cool, crisp mornings, the frost on the ground and the fog hanging over the landscape. It is relaxing to breathe in the pleasant outdoor aroma on a quiet afternoon. The display of reds and oranges from the hardwoods mixed with the yellows of the softer woods, along with the green in the evergreens, paint scenery far beyond what any picture can capture.

I enjoy the outdoors. The stress of my work world disappears quickly when I'm out in God's world. Nothing can compare to watching one part of the world wake up and the other get ready for bed as the sun rises and falls on the horizon. As my hunting dog locks up on point, I am astonished by his keen sense of smell. It's exhilarating to watch that flock of waterfowl make their last turn and begin to rock on their descent or to catch a glimpse of a grouse drumming for his mate on a log. There are few situations that can cause my heart to pound more than hearing a twig snap in the woods as a doe or buck appears and few greater challenges than calling a gobbler into range.

Despite the anticipation I feel when I put on my camouflage and make way into the woods, I have an even stronger passion than hunting. I want to see outdoors people connect, or reconnect, with God. God has changed my life in so many positive ways and I want others to experience those pleasant changes also. I would like to assist you in discovering a new view of life which will enable you to experience more beauty in God's great outdoors.

The following pages are true stories taken out of my own hunting experiences, as best as I recall. Many of these have been shared with my kids. Those are some of the best memories I have with them. I'm yet to find a better mentoring atmosphere than hunting together. I have enjoyed allowing them to take friends along. Why not share our enjoyment with others? It doesn't lessen, but expands our fun. Some of my deepest friendships with adults have been formed in the out of doors. What better place to build a friendship than in a sport that we both enjoy.

These "Insights for Living from a Seasoned Hunter" are designed to help you relate an outdoor situation to a principle from the Bible. I trust that these stories will encourage and inspire you, but also help you to reflect on your relationship with God. Enjoy reading and sense more deeply how God is at work in our world.

Calling Deer

It was my favorite location for bow hunting. I was in a tree overlooking a gate at a four corners location. To my right behind me was a cornfield, on my left running behind me was an alfalfa field, in front and on the right was a woods, and ahead on the left was a bean field. I had previously seen deer in all of these areas. Behind the alfalfa field was a bigger woods and swamp area that usually held a real nice buck and some other deer. Sitting in this location, I once had a little button buck come right up to my tree and stand on his back legs and smell every tree step. He was ready to reach up to my boot when suddenly his mother must have called him, because he went running to his mother and snuggled up to her side.

It was a great evening. I had gotten into my stand early and was enjoying the fresh air and a light fall breeze. The trees were just starting to change colors. Suddenly I saw him come out...about 100 yards away a nice 8 pointer came out with his nose to the ground! I slowly moved my deer call to my lips — I had it adjusted between a young and adult buck. I blew the call a couple of times. At first the buck didn't seem to notice, he was so intent on some smell he was following. After the third call I made, he suddenly turned and came RUNNING my way. He ran at a fast pace right at me until he was about 40 yards away when he slowed down a little bit. A couple of more calls kept him coming right at me. He was looking quite upset and ready to fight whatever buck had moved into his territory! He

God

is

calling

you

kept coming until he was right below my tree. I was at full draw, but waited for two more steps when he would be broadside at about 10 yards right in the open gateway. Suddenly he just exploded sideways - he must have gotten a scent. I have never seen a deer jump so far straight sideways, but he landed in the brush at the edge of the woods and quickly disappeared. Why didn't I take the shot sooner? I waited too long. I decided to use my deer call a couple of times, but figured I had blown my chance.

A little while later (it seemed like an hour), the buck came out again, right where he had at first again with his nose down. He was following the same scent out into the bean field. I tried calling again, not expecting a response, but immediately he came on the run again! This time, though, he was more cautious and swung wide of my tree, too far for a good shot.

I now live with one of those "should have's" - I should have taken the shot when he was right below me instead of waiting for two more steps that didn't happen. I have a tendency not to wait long enough, but this time I waited too long.

I have enjoyed calling deer. Sometimes I don't see any response. And I also have seen nice bucks turn and run away; later I found out there was a monster buck in the area that was beating up even on a huge 10 point, so no wonder the smaller deer ran away when I called.

I even had one scary experience calling. I was walking out one night and heard a buck grunting just inside the edge of the woods. I was walking out on the perimeter of the cornfield next to the woods, so just for fun, I started to call wondering if this buck would respond. It sounded like a real young buck as it had a rather weak, "wimpy" grunt. I grunted a couple of times and could hear this deer moving closer to me. Suddenly I looked up and saw a huge deer charging right at me. At the same time as he was charging me, I heard this wimpy grunt come out into the edge of the corn right behind me. I realized I was between two deer coming to fight off the buck that had gotten into their territory! I watched the big deer come charging until he got about 20 yards away, then he stopped and started pawing the ground and snorting and grunting like he was really upset. I figured that was close enough! It wasn't light enough for a good shot and it was after legal shooting hours anyway. I started waving my arms, and both deer stopped, snorted, pawed the ground, and then bolted away. I've decided to be more cautious with calling deer after that experience.

When I think of calling deer, I am reminded that someone else is calling us. God is calling us. He says:

"Come to me, all who are weary and burdened, and I will give you rest."

God is calling us into a right relationship with himself. He is offering a better lifestyle. He wants to take away our load of guilt and shame — forgive us through Jesus Christ! He offers us a better life now and in the future.

Have you responded to his call? Or are you too distracted by the other things around you. The stakes are high. The call is real. Why don't you go running to God and see what he has to offer you!

And for those of us who have responded to him, we may need to respond again. Even that first buck was willing to come back a second time when I called. Perhaps life has become very difficult for you. Stress

Will you come?

has reached a high peak in your life or perhaps you have messed up and are living with the consequences. Remember what Jesus says:

"Come to me, all who are weary and burdened, and I will give you rest."

Inner peace, calmness, relaxed, at ease, forgiven, restored.

Will you come?

Bible
Reference
Matthew
11:28

Additional
Reading
Matthew
11:28--30

H eavy Fog

Early morning often seems to be one of the best times for hunting, especially big game, like the whitetail deer. But in a place like here in Michigan, especially in early season bow hunting, we often find a heavy fog over the land.

Sometimes that fog can be so thick that it is hard to even see where we are going. We strain to see the edge of the road as we go out to our hunting spot. It's a lot harder to find our tree stand, as the fog seems to engulf us. We can see such a short distance ahead of us through such a soupy mess. Perhaps you are a waterfowl hunter. You experience fog as you travel to your area, but also see the mist over the lake as you set your decoys.

I think life is often like that, religiously. People often live in a fog. God doesn't seem very clear or real to them.

I think of a man whose name was Ed. For years God was sort of off in the fog for him. Ed believed in a supreme being. He believed there was some power behind the universe but that's about all. He didn't see God very clearly and didn't have a very close relationship with him.

Ed started out in a fog, a rather heavy fog, but the fog gradually began to lift and the sun began to shine (I should say Son began to shine) in his life. He gradually

Are you living in a fog?

discovered that God was very real and that God was inviting him to share in a close, personal relationship.

He saw what God had to offer – love, forgiveness, peace, purpose, more meaningful friendships.

As the fog lifted Ed at first felt guilty and ashamed, as he considering his own life and the way he had been living. He certainly didn't have an acceptable mix to offer up to God, but then he became so overwhelmed by the love he sensed and he began to experience the forgiveness that God offers.

God seems unclear

He realized that Jesus had paid the penalty for all his failures. He put his trust in Jesus Christ and invited him to come into his life, by his Spirit, to lead him in a new direction.

Perhaps you have been living in a fog. God seems so unclear. There must be a higher being of some sort, but God seems so far off.

It's my prayer that the fog will lift and you will see God more clearly and see what he is offering you. I urge you to strain through the fog, just like when you are driving. You strain, search, try to find the edge of the road. Seek God, try to find him. God says:

> "You will seek me and find me when you seek me with all your heart."

I urge you to seek the Lord with all your heart. Seriously consider, see if God is real. Try to find him. Ask him to make himself known to you if he exists.

Bible Reference Jeremiah 29:13

18

F lashlights

It was opening morning for bowhunting. We had our tree stands in the woods. Now all we had to do was get up early and go to the woods. I had gotten permission from their schools to take two of my boys out with me. We woke up early and got dressed to head out. We had a little breakfast, planning on our good hunter's meal after we returned.

As we were getting ready to leave, I checked with my boys to make sure they had a flashlight along. My one boy did, but the other one did not. I had one extra, so I let him take the pick between the two that I had. He chose one and I could use the other.

My boys and I left to go to the woods. When we got there I parked our car along the side of the road. We got out, got our bows out of their cases, got our backpacks out, and were ready to head out into the woods.

My boys took out their flashlights, and I reached for mine. Suddenly I realized that my light was back at the cottage; I had left it on the table (I guess "old age" is starting to set in). I decided to walk to my tree stand without a light. We were on private land (if it would have been gun hunting, I would have gone back as I always use a flashlight for safety during gun seasons) and I had my tree stand in the same location as last year, so I thought I could find it.

Jesus

the

Light

of the

World

When we first started out, it wasn't bad at all. The moon was out and we were walking across an open field, plus my boys had flashlights and used them when we needed them. We also had to cross a stream, so it was very helpful to have a flashlight at that point so we would not get wet feet before we started hunting.

After we crossed the stream, we each walked separately to our stands. One boy went one way, the other went the other, and I headed almost straight ahead.

As I left the boys, I still didn't have much trouble, as we were still in a clearing, but it didn't take long and I would have to go into the woods. It is amazing how dark it gets in the woods during early season with all the leaves on the trees. Even though I had my tree stand in the same location last year, it was very difficult to try to find my tree without a flashlight. Eventually, and I might add, after spooking a deer, I found my tree.

We hunted a few hours (of course that deer didn't return after I spooked it and probably informed the others I was there also), and returned to camp for our special "hunter's breakfast."

About mid-afternoon we went back to our stands again to sit until evening. That time I made sure I had my flashlight, as I would need it to get out, especially to cross the stream. One thing I noticed, it didn't take me long at all to find my stand in the light. I had no problem finding my tree with the sun shining and it being light out.

As I thought about this, I remembered a verse from the Bible. Jesus is speaking and he makes a claim about himself. He says:

"I am the light of the world."

If you think about it, we live in a rather dark, gloomy world. We hear about all kinds of trouble and turbulence in our world, floods and earthquakes. Every news broadcast reminds us of conflict between people, wars and fighting in different areas. But even closer to home we have murders and violence, and many other problems.

In our own lives, life often seems so dark...like trying to find our way in a woods in the dark. Confusion and doubt, loneliness and fear, brokenness and problems, guilt and shame, unanswered questions. Jesus claims:

"I am the light of the world."

He's saying, I am like the sun in your spiritual world. If you have a right relationship with me, I will light up your dark world.

In my own life, since I have connected to Jesus I have found this to be true: Jesus lights up my world. Not all questions are answered, but life does make more sense. I find purpose and fulfillment. Relationships improve when we live God's way. I know God loves me and I have peace inside, because I know I am forgiven.

Jesus does make a real difference. It's more like living in the light instead of walking in a dark woods. It's like having a bright flashlight to help us find our way.

Have you found how he can light up your life or must you investigate this claim more?

Bible Reference John 8:12

Additional Reading Psalm 119:115

An Embarrassing Miss!

Missing

the

Target

=

Sin

It was opening morning for gun deer. We had gotten out early and set up our portable blind underneath a pine tree near a scrape line. I had my youngest boy with me in the blind. He helped me set it up and helped clear away a few branches so we could see better and hopefully I could get a good shot.

It all worked well. We were hidden behind this leafy type blind material, so we didn't have to sit perfectly still. I have enjoyed taking my children out and have tried to make it as easy as possible for them to see game and be involved in the action even when they were too young to shoot.

As it was getting light, a deer started moving up the runway working his scrape line. It didn't take long to see that it was a buck. I did not focus on the antlers, but I could easily see that it had a massive rack! I nudged my boy and pointed toward the deer. He knew what to do now – sit still and not make a noise. I slowly lifted my rifle when the deer was feeding, so he wouldn't notice the movement. To make things easier, there was a little crotch of a branch right next to my gun, so I gently laid the gun there for a rest.

I was watching this big buck move closer and closer. He shouldn't scent us from the angle he was coming in. He was still in some thick brush, so I didn't want to risk a shot yet, but he was now easily within range. He kept coming our way; soon he would be out in the open.

I watched him through my scope. I carefully checked to see when he would be in the open. I did not want to repeat a previous experience of hitting a branch between the deer and me.

He stepped right out into the open at about 75 yards. I laid the crosshairs of my scope right on his kill zone. I looked through the scope again and everything looked clear. I gently squeezed the trigger and my 30-06 rang out loudly.

But something strange happened. The blind material that we had hung around us went flying! The deer stood there for a moment, surprised by the noise, but obviously not hit, and then turned and scampered into the thick brush.

What happened? How could I have missed? There was nothing between the deer and me. I had carefully checked through the scope. But I made a mistake. I only looked through the scope and didn't see a large branch right in front of my barrel that was too close to see through the scope! My son could see it, but he thought I would notice it and he didn't dare move or make a noise. To make matters even more embarrassing, the branch that I hit was holding up our blind, so the whole blind went flying when I shot.

Needless to say my son still talks about this miss (and it is not the only miss he can talk about) and the big buck that got away.

Embarrassing miss. Almost all are and every hunter knows what it is like. We miss the target. Whether it is just in practice shooting a round of skeet, trap, trying to score in sporting clays, or whether it is at an archery range. It's usually more embarrassing to miss in the field, but we all have done that too. The pheasant continues to fly even though we know it must be dead. The deer (or those several deer) that out jumped the arrow or avoided the bullet. Waterfowl, upland game, big game – chalk up misses. We have all been there.

Missing the target. That's how the Bible describes SIN. Missing the target that God sets up on how we ought to live.

We have all missed God's target. Sometimes this has been very embarrassing. The Bible says:

"...for all have sinned and fall short of the glory of God,"

Sin causes guilt and shame and produces many other consequences. Even worse than that there is a penalty for sin.

"For the wages of sin is death;"

Which means separation from God – HELL. But the GOOD NEWS of the Bible is that God doesn't leave us here.

Our children may tell and retell the story of our misses. God has a better plan. He loves us enough that he wants to forgive us!

"If we confess our sins, he is faithful and just and will forgive our sins and purify us from all unrighteousness."

God will not only forgive – pardon us, He also will

clean us up on the inside and give us a brand new start. But we need to admit that we have sinned, own up to our failures, and ask God to forgive us.

Today spend some time admitting to God where you have failed, or better yet, make a list on a sheet of paper (don't show it to anyone) and when you are finished, prayerfully ask God to forgive each one listed and the others you didn't list or that you did not think of. Take the paper and tear up your sheet and throw it away, remembering God's promise to forgive you.

Bible
Reference
Romans
3:23; 6:23;
I John 1:9

Tree Stand in a Wrong Location

Pursuing

wrong

goals

results

in

problems

I suspect every bowhunter has had a time when your treestand was in the wrong location. No matter how hard you scouted, how much you studied the patterns, how carefully you checked the wind direction; you still were sitting in the wrong location. The buck came in 50 or 75 yards over to the side of where you were sitting.

Several times I have experienced having my tree stand in the wrong location, even when I thought I had chosen the best location. The bucks seemed to have a different idea about where they chose to be. I remember one day I was in my stand. It was late afternoon on a beautiful fall day. After I arrived at my stand, I sat quietly for some time just in case something was nearby and had heard me coming. After some time, I decided to try my grunt call. Almost immediately I saw a nice 8-point swing out of a swamp near me. He went downwind, just as I expected. I apparently had covered my scent well enough, because he was not spooked. He started working up my way. My heart began to pound. As he came closer, he swung out wide. I thought I had things patterned right, but that buck never got in range. It was an interesting evening watching him totally destroy some bushes nearby. If only I had placed my stand about 25 yards over, I would have had a good shot, but I was up the wrong tree. He was out of range.

I think that experience parallels situations in our lives. We often have our treestand up in the wrong location so we miss out on the good things in life. Think about how many people have pursued goals that destroyed some of the best things in their lives. At the time, they thought financial gain was all important, or a career move; but in the process their marriage fell apart, they lost good contact with their kids, previous friends were no longer considered friends, and we could go on from there. The Bible says:

"The thief comes only to steal and kill and destroy;"

That refers to what Satan tries to do in our lives. He gets us focused in the wrong place, like sitting in the wrong tree in life, and we miss out on the best things. But Jesus went on to say:

"I have come that they may have life, and have it to the full."

In fact the word he used describes a life so full of good things that it overflows. Connecting with Jesus, living life his way, and fitting into his purpose and plan is the most satisfying, rewarding life possible. Not only do we have inner peace, joy, meaning, and purpose; we bond with others around us in more positive ways, and enjoy better relationships.

Think about your life. Are you sitting in the wrong tree? You might see some good things happen at a distance, but they are not a part of your lifestyle. Perhaps you have already experienced some of the brokenness and problems of having your focus directed in the wrong place. Come to Jesus. He offers forgiveness as well as a new and better life!

A relationship with Jesus brings a better life

Bible Reference John 10:10

A View from A Treestand

Ugly

scars

remind

us of

our

scarred

lives

Sitting in a treestand in late afternoon offers lots of time for thinking and observing before deer begin to move toward evening. It's possible to see a deer early, but usually it just means getting in position for a possible shot later in the evening. I suspect many outdoors people do some refocusing during this time.

One afternoon I had gotten out early. It was a beautiful day with pleasant temperatures and not much wind. I was in one of my "permanent" stands and knew the patterns quite well, so I figured I would have a significant wait before I would see a deer.

As I was looking around from my stand I began to focus on the trees around me. Most of them are very tall old trees with lots of room underneath. Because of the canopy of leaves up above, few lower branches survived over the years. In their place were some ugly scars where the branches had been.

As I looked up, I could see some healthy green leaves up high, beautiful branches reaching out in various directions. The trees were swaying gently in the breeze, but down below were these ugly scars in the bark.

As I reflected on that, it made me think of our lives. At the first glance, we are more like the tops of the trees – lots of life and branching out in many different areas. But if we are honest, all of us have some ugly scars from our past. I'm not talking about a scar from a

28

surgery or from some laceration, but instead scars from the stupid choices we made and from the sins we committed. Some of the trees even had a distorted twist after some of the scars where it looked like a branch blew off in the wind. Many of us have had to adjust life because of some choices we made and we may still be living with the consequences. I think of a man who talked to me and told me how he spent too much time on his job and his marriage fell apart which he deeply regretted. I think of another person who got caught up in using too much alcohol and his whole life fell apart and he spent years rebuilding the pieces. We all have made stupid, wrong choices and we may still be struggling with the consequences of these.

The Bible talks about this. It says:

"There is no one righteous, not even one."

We all have some messed up spots in our past (and even in our present). We do not like to focus on this aspect of our lives. It is easier to focus on the good things happening now instead of the blunders that we have made in the past, but it is important that we deal with our mistakes instead of just ignoring them.

The Bible not only accurately describes our condition, but it also gives us a solution for change. It shows us how God can apply some good pruning paint on the ugly scars of our lives. God is willing to forgive us, but we need to acknowledge our sin and ask for his forgiveness.

"If we confess our sins, he is faithful and just and will forgive us our sins..."

Take some time to review your life and be honest about the mistakes you made. If you have not asked for God's forgiveness in the past, then make sure you get this matter settled with him. If you know you have already been forgiven, let the ugly scar be a reminder of how good God is and make sure you thank him again.

Bible
Reference
Romans
3:10
I John 1:9

Additional
Reading
Romans
3:9-12

S tepping on a Dead Branch

It seems like no matter how careful I am walking out to my treestand, I invariably step on some dead wood, especially if I am going out for an early morning hunt. My stand provides a good place for a morning hunt; it is located between where deer feed and where they rest. I must be very quiet though as I move to the stand because the deer often start moving into my area as soon as it starts getting light or even before.

I remember a time last fall. I was heading out to my stand carefully picking my way to avoid making noise. I crossed the beaver dam, proceeded through a small clump of trees, out across the clearing and finally I was getting right near my stand in the edge of the next group of trees.

I spotted the pine tree at the entrance and moved slowly forward. I was about halfway there when suddenly, crunch! I had stepped on a dead branch! It sounded like the whole forest rang out with noise. I looked up as I heard the snort of a deer and watched a nice buck leaving with his antlers gleaming in the moonlight. Needless to say, my hunt was not successful that morning.

Dead wood. There really is a lot of it in the woods. Lots of dead branches lying on the ground. Dead trees still standing or tipped over. I hunt near a swamp which includes lots of dead trees.

We are "dead" in our trespasses and sins

A relationship with Jesus brings life

The Bible talks about being "dead." It says this about us:

"As for you, you were dead in your transgressions and sins,"

As far as God is concerned, we cannot do anything good that impresses him. We are like dead wood, useless, good only for firewood. But God's prescription goes beyond this dreadful diagnosis; he offers a good remedy. We can be made alive in a relationship with Jesus Christ. The Bible says:

"But because of his great love for us, God, who is rich in mercy, made us alive with Christ..."

It then goes on to tell us that this is by grace, a gift from God. We need to have a personal relationship with Jesus Christ, which comes by putting our trust in him and inviting him, by his spirit, to come into our lives and lead us.

The next time you step on a dead branch or see a dead limb on a tree or a dead tree, remember that we who were "dead in sin" can be "alive" through a relationship with Jesus Christ.

Bible
Reference
Ephesians
2:1
2:5,6

Additional
Reading
Ephesians
2:1-10

A Pleasant Surprise

One day I received a phone call from someone who had attended our Sportsperson's Club. He had found a bag that contained three picture albums. The person who called had come to some of our seminars and thought he had seen one of the people pictured at a seminar, but he couldn't remember his name, so he brought the picture albums over to me.

As soon as I looked through the albums, I could see that they were some very important pictures: years of photos of different hunts, awards received at the National Wild Turkey Federation, group hunts, individual hunts, a woman who was successful in turkey hunting, and other important people pictured.

I called the person who seemed to be featured in many of the pictures. He immediately admitted he had lost them. It was rather embarrassing as he had put the bag up on top of his vehicle and drove off with it up there. When he got to his destination he discovered that he had lost all these valuable pictures.

He said he prayed that they would be returned. He went back up and down the road where he had driven, and could not find them. All he could find along the road were trash containers out for the garbage pickup. He could only assume that someone had picked these albums up and thrown them in the trash.

When I called him, all he could say was that it was a

We deserve eternal punishment

miracle that someone found them and got them back to him. He thought they were lost forever.

Isn't that a lot like our lives? Without even realizing it, we are lost spiritually. We have drifted away from God. We have lived in such a way that puts a separation between God and us.

We have sinned and fallen short of what God expects, and we are headed toward the garbage dump.

God

That's like an expression that Jesus used in the Bible. It was like he pointed over to the garbage pit of Jerusalem, **has** which was called GEHENNA, and said, 'If you want to know what hell is like, look over there.' In those **provided** days they didn't bury their garbage, they burned it. He described Hell like that – that continual place of burning **a free** where the fire never goes out. If we are honest we are headed in that direction:

gift of

"For the wages of sin is death,"

salvation

This means eternal death, separation from God, Hell. BUT THE MIRACLE IS that we can be found, saved! The wages of sin is death.

"...but the gift of God is eternal life in Christ Jesus our Lord."

Just as this person had to reach out and accept the package with his valuable pictures in it, so too, you and I won't have a new and better life with a fantastic future unless we ACCEPT the gift of God.

You can do that simply like this: honestly, personally, tell God in your own words. Admit that you are a sinner. Tell Jesus that you believe in him. You put your trust in him. You believe he suffered and died to pay the penalty for your sin. Invite him to come into your life, by his Spirit, and ask him to lead your life. If you have never done that, why not right now in a quiet prayer talk to God.

The stakes are high. Normally we would end up in an awful garbage dump – Hell. But because of God's love and miraculous intervention we can have a better life now and look forward to heaven in the future.

Bible
Reference
Romans
3:23, 6:23

Additional
Reading
I John 1:9;
John 1:12

Duck Hunting
- No Excuses!

It was the fall of the year and the early duck season had begun in Iowa. Teal were moving through the area, so it should be a good hunt. I was scheduled to meet some friends at a favorite hunting spot. This place was a swampy slough about 10 miles from where I lived.

One of my friends had just moved back into the state and this was our first time hunting together. I had the decoys. He had a canoe. We could use the canoe to put out the decoys and retrieve any birds we shot. We set up in a larger section of water putting out about three dozen decoys and waited for it to get light.

As it got light we noticed that there were a couple of other hunters across the lake. They were well out of range, so it wasn't dangerous but we could see they had a massive display of decoys. Hundreds of decoys stretched out over the water. Would we have any chance with that many decoys on the other side of the pond?

Eventually some ducks started to move and we began calling but were also joined in calling by the other hunters across the lake. It seemed like all the ducks were attracted to the other side of the pond with the massive display of decoys; there was a lot of shooting over there. Eventually a few ducks moved our way and we got in on the action too.

We shot one and it landed out beyond our decoys so my friend decided to retrieve it with his canoe. As he was out there retrieving it, he noticed that one of the other hunters was on a wild chase with a duck he had crippled. It was a diver and every time he would get near it with his duck boat the duck would dive and swim away.

He was chasing that duck further and further our way. My friend retrieved our duck and then noticed the other person's duck come up right near him so he killed it, retrieved it, and brought it over to this other hunter. The hunter thanked him for his help.

My friend paddled back to shore, but the other hunter followed him in his duck boat to our blind. I thought it was a little strange. Why was he coming over to our blind? We had just helped him; we had just retrieved the duck that he couldn't catch. He certainly wouldn't be checking on how we were doing. He could see and had asked my friend about that already. Our little display of decoys told the story compared to their large, massive display.

My friend got out of the canoe and tucked it back out of sight. The other man ran his duck boat right up on shore and walked over to my friend who had just helped him. Then he pulled out a badge. "Let me see the registration for that canoe."

"Registration? It's not registered. I was told that it did not have to be registered."

"But you were just using it in the water and the law says it has to be registered before you can use it."

"I just moved here. Where we lived before we did not need to have it registered. When we moved here I went to the local sporting goods and checked and they told

Ignorance

of the

law

is no

excuse

me that I didn't have to have the canoe registered as long as I didn't use a motor on it, and you can see I don't have a motor on it."

"I don't know who you talked to or where he got his information but the information you received is not accurate. You need to register that canoe whether or not you have a motor on it. If you put it on public waters it needs to be registered."

Eventually he wrote up a citation. I think it cost my friend a lot of money.

In the same way, ignorance of spiritual matters does not excuse us from the penalties attached to living incorrectly! Being ignorant does not provide you with a legitimate excuse when you face God on the final judgment day if you have not connected with Him in the proper way here on this earth.

In the Bible God reveals himself to us first through the beautiful world that he has made and then more clearly through the Bible. The Bible teaches us how we can be right with God and how he wants us to live.

God also explains in the Bible the consequences of not relating with him properly; consequences now – a more miserable, broken, messed up lifestyle - and the penalty in the future – Hell. To be uninformed is not a legitimate excuse. Listen to what God says in the Bible:

Bible
Reference
Romans
1:20

"...so that men are without excuse."

I urge you to get to know what God says. Read the Bible. The book of Romans goes on to clearly show us how to be right with God. If you need help, ask a Christian to help you. Attend a Bible-believing church. Ignorance of the law is no excuse.

Additional
Reading
Romans
1:18-32

R ecovering a Bow Shot Deer

One of the most important factors of recovering a bow shot deer is finding a good blood trail. Even with a good hit, a deer usually runs some distance in a short time before it dies making it difficult to find. Even when one sees where the arrow hits, it still is encouraging to find a good blood trail that one can follow.

I remember the excitement of seeing a good blood trail after shooting a nice buck. It was just before dark, so we waited for about an hour. Then our kids were able to have the enjoyment of tracking at night with lanterns, looking for a deer. That can prove to be an interesting experience by itself, and it is so fascinating to watch blood spots appear in lantern light.

Blood is an important concept in the Bible. In earlier history there were a variety of blood sacrifices that people used in religious ceremonies. They saw how closely blood related to life and death. Shedding the blood of an animal symbolized the payment for sin so that forgiveness could be reached.

In the New Testament we read about the shedding of blood also, the precious blood of Jesus Christ. When he suffered and died and shed his blood, he paid the penalty for our sin and satisfied the justice of God.

"For you know that it was not with perishable things such as silver or gold that you were redeemed from

Without the shedding of blood there is no forgiveness

the empty way of life handed down to you from your forefathers, but with the precious blood of Christ, a lamb without blemish or defect."

God could have chosen another method, but this is what would satisfy his justice.

"...and without the shedding of blood there is no forgiveness."

Are you trying to connect with God through your own efforts? You will never make it. If you accept the sacrifice of Jesus Christ through which he shed his blood for you, for your forgiveness, you will be changed. You will no longer experience the empty lifestyle; a new and better way of living will be yours.

As you reflect on the importance of a trail of blood to recover a bow shot whitetail, may you even more deeply ponder the significance of Jesus' blood trail shed for your forgiveness.

Bible
Reference
I Peter
1:18,19;
Hebrews
9:22

40

Hunting Camp

Some of our most memorable times of hunting have been in sharing time with family members or friends.

I think of a duck hunting experience we had a couple of years ago. We drove through the night after my son's football game and went to a lodge on Saginaw Bay. In the morning they took us out to one of their blinds, a pontoon boat made into a very comfortable blind for my boys, our dog, and myself. It was not a good day for hunting. The weather had been and was too nice for duck hunting and the Northern migrations had not really begun even though it was getting late in the season. We were able to shoot a couple of ducks, but nothing like anticipated. But did that mean that we had a bad day? Absolutely not. It was a day that stands out in our memory as a very pleasant time together. Hunting in a blind with my three sons, it can't get much better than that!

How often we hear people talking about "huntin camp." Often there isn't that much discussion about what deer or other game was taken, unless perhaps someone got a nice wall hanger. But there is something special about hunting camp with buddies. For us it is good clean fun and friendship. Good meals together, sharing stories, and laughing a lot. We recap the day's hunt and plan for the next. We adjust strategy depending upon what happened during the day.

Friends and family, that's what it means to be a Christian!

Friendship in the family of God

The Bible says:

"Yet to all who received him, to those who believed in his name, he gave the right to become children of God"

That makes us brothers and sisters in God's family. The Bible says in another place:

"How great is the love the Father has lavished on us that we should be called children of God! And that is what we are!"

Amazing, that God is willing to adopt us as children when we "receive and believe."

Not only do we have access to the best "Daddy," we also can enjoy some of the most wonderful relationships with other members in His family. One great benefit of being a Christian is belonging to this caring family. As Christians we rejoice together and we suffer together. We encourage each other and pray for each other. We are still human and we make mistakes in how we relate to others, but I have found that some of the most meaningful relationships exist between Christians.

Are you a member of God's family? If so, that means we are a part of the same family! If not, why would you want to miss out of some of the most meaningful relationships that exist?

Bible
Reference
John 1:12;
I John 3:1,2

L istening for a Twig to Snap

I suspect many of us who bowhunt try to listen carefully for a twig to snap.

It's a nice day. You get out of work early or it's Saturday afternoon and you decide to sit in your stand until dark. Arriving early — you want to be in your stand well before deer movement begins, so that you won't disturb anything walking in. It is a pleasant afternoon. It is cool and the sun is shining. You carefully take your equipment out of the car and walk into the woods keeping yourself disguised as much as possible. As you arrive at your tree, you selectively put some scent in appropriate places. You review your equipment and finally climb your tree. Once on your stand you get situated. You check out your markers for distance, just to be sure. You know it might be a couple of hours before deer begin to move, but it's possible you might see one earlier.

Be still

and

know

that

I am

God

Once you are settled in your stand, you carefully look around becoming very familiar with the surroundings so that you can detect any movement or anything new or out of the ordinary. You sit very still and make slow movements. You strain your ears to listen intently for any new sound. You try to get accustomed to the noises of the woods so that you detect any new sound. You listen intently, waiting especially for that twig to snap.

We might get excited and our heart beat a little faster when we hear the leaves rustle, but we know a squirrel can make that kind of noise. Only a heavier animal like a deer can snap a twig, break a dead branch lying on the ground, or better yet, a buck snap a branch above a scrape he has just visited. Be still, listen for that twig to snap. The Bible talks about being still:

"Be still, and know that I am God."

Stop what you are doing. Slow down, quiet yourself, and realize that I AM GOD!

How often we keep such a busy pace. We seem to be on a constant run, go go go. We do so many things; our appointments books are filled. Not only our own schedules are, but if we have a family there are all those events to attend. With long hours at work and over time, plus other activities there seems to be so little time left.

It seems like each day begins with the treadmill of life already running fast and we need to jump on and start running. And we run all day and come home tired (or all night, if we work the night shift). The Bible says — be still, slow down, quiet yourself.

Get somewhere, some place where you can be still and then in that stillness think about God. In that quietness — do some soul searching, do some evaluation, do some reflecting.

In that quietness in your heart come to know, to realize, to experience that God is real! Realize he is calling us into a new or renewed relationship with him. Be quiet, listen intently — for the spiritual twig to snap.

Be still and know that He is God.

Bible
Reference
Psalm 46:10

44

C ompass Makes the Difference

I recall deer hunting one time when I was younger. I was with a group of older hunters. We were hunting up in Northern Michigan in the Dead Stream Swamp area (even the name has a scary ring to it). I haven't been up there recently, but my recollection as a teenager is that one would not want to get lost in that area. You could walk for miles before you would get out and it is a very difficult swamp to get through.

The adults decided to do a drive for deer. A couple of the older hunters organized the drive and each of us headed to the designated areas. It was late in the afternoon and this swamp was rather large, but we felt we had just enough time to cover it. We proceeded on the drive wandering back and forth around the water holes. I believe we saw one deer but could not get a shot at it. Eventually we came across a small clearing with a small hill in the center "behind" this large swamp. It was starting to get dark. We met together and would be heading back. I was not too concerned, because the older hunters had hunted in that area before.

My feelings began to change though when I heard one of the older hunters ask another, "Which direction do you think is North?" I watched him point in a direction that did not seem right to me. The first hunter said, "No, I thought it was that way," and he pointed the opposite direction. About that time a third experienced hunter joined them and they asked him what direction was North - and he pointed in a different direction than

The Bible

makes a

difference

in our

lives

the other two. It was overcast, so we couldn't see which way the sun was setting.

Three experienced hunters all pointing in different directions and it is getting dark in the dead stream swamp area! Finally one of them asked, "Does any one here have a compass?" No one had a compass except for me. I had a real cheap one and I did not know if it was trust worthy or not. I had picked it up at something like a "Dollar" store, so I hesitated even showing them, because I didn't know how reliable it would be, but since they did not seem to know which way we should go, I showed them what I had. I am sure they were not very impressed with the quality (lack of it), but they took it and looked at which way it pointed.

Finally, one of the more experienced hunters said, "This does not seem right, but we do not agree on what is North, so let's follow the compass." He concluded that we were about a mile from the road based on the amount of time we had spent walking. He said, "I will lead and follow this compass and go in a straight line." He told one of the other men to count how many steps we were taking, figuring 1760 yards in a mile, he estimated that we need to go about 1900 steps. This persons could let us know when we had traveled a mile. He then said that if we went that far and didn't find the road, we would have to repeat this procedure in a different direction until we found the road.

We followed our leader step by step. In those dense dark woods, it seemed to be getting dark very fast! Some of the night sounds were sounding a little more scary than usual. The leader followed tree after tree in a straight line checking the compass as he went. One of the other men counted step by step as we proceeded. When we reached the number of steps he had estimated we ended up about 10 feet from the middle of the road where we wanted to be and were not very far from where we had parked our cars! One little inexpensive compass had guided us correctly!

Now I will not go into a new hunting area, especially if it is a very large area, with out having a very good compass. In fact, I always have a compass in my backpack, and have found it to be very helpful (especially in trying to recover a bow shot deer at night).

Life is often like the experience that we had. We think we know our way. Even older, mature adults seem to think they know the right direction. But if you compared plans you would find some major differences. Things seem to be going quite well. Life seems to be making sense, but then some darkness settles in. A relationship begins to get stretched or falls apart. Finances seem to crumble. The job situation goes from bad to worse. We are "up on the hill at the end of the swamp" wondering what direction is north.

Do you ever feel that way, like life is not really making good sense? Are you wondering if there is a God? And if there is why is the world in such a mess? Are you facing some of the hurt and fears and failures in your own life?

Then it's time to turn to a compass; this compass is the Bible. It can give us new direction. It can help us make sense out of life. It can guide us into improved relationships. It can help us to connect with God properly. Listen to some of the things the Bible can do for us.

"Your word is a lamp to our feet and a light for my path"

"How can a young man keep his way pure? By living according to your word."

"I have hidden your word in my heart that I might not sin against you."

The Bible tells us how it is helpful in the following ways: It can revive us. Ever get down or feel discouraged? The Bible can refresh us. It makes us wise and helps us to make smart decisions. It brings joy to our hearts. It enlightens us. The Bible is dependable. We can count on God doing what he says. It says refering to God's instructions:

"...in keeping them there is great reward."

These are just a few thoughts of how helpful the Bible can be in our daily life. Turn to the Bible, the best compass, which can lead us in the right direction!

Bible
Reference
Psalm
119:105,
10,11

Additional
Reading
Psalm 19;
119:9

Hunter Safety

For the last several years our Sportsperson's Club has been teaching hunter safety.

We have several certified instructors including myself. In the last few years we have had many students come through our courses.

The

Bible

is very

useful

for

safe

living

During the 12 hours of instruction a variety of topics are covered, but all deal with safety. Some are focused on safe gun handling; others are directed more toward safety in bow hunting; and others deal with survival skills; and we also include a simulated field course. Although this is a required course, most students seem eager to learn so that they can begin hunting.

In hunter safety there is a manual that we cover very carefully during the course. There is another manual that many of us neglect. It was also designed for our safety; safe living now and safety in the future. This manual is the Bible.

The Bible can do many things for us. It can teach us the best way to live. It can help us to understand when we go off the track. It can give us instructions for how to get back on the right road. It can provide us with the equipment for living in the right way.

"All Scripture is God-breathed."

The Bible isn't just another good book. It is a very special book given to us by God himself. It is his word. He breathed it out by his Spirit and people wrote it down.

"and is useful for teaching, rebuking, correcting and training in righteousness so that the man of God may be thoroughly equipped for every good work."

Each student is willing and eager to learn safe practices for hunting. Are we more concerned about how we can live safely and how we can be safe in the future?

The Bible will help us in this way.

Bible
Reference
II Timothy
3:15, 16

M arked Trail

One thing that helps me a lot when I am hunting is my flashlight. It is very difficult to find one's way in dark woods without a light, especially in early season when there are a lot of leaves on the trees. But I also "cheat" a little. I not only use my flashlight, but I use a marked trail.

I purchase some of these twist ties or reflector dots that I can tie on a branch or push into a tree. Before the season starts, I mark my way into the woods to my treestands.

Light

for

living

It is amazing how a flashlight and a tiny reflector strip or dot can make a major difference in getting to a tree stand. It is so much easier to find our way out of the woods in the evening, because we have a spot marked where we need to cross the stream.

I also find a flashlight helpful for safety reasons. Even though I hunt on private land, I cannot be assured that there is not a person there who might be careless and shoot at some noise or movement in the dark. This is especially true in gun hunting, but also can be true in bowhunting. Turning a flashlight on and pointing it down or using it occasionally would let anyone know that a someone is coming and would not frighten deer.

Did you know that the Bible is like a flashlight, in this way? The psalmist says:

"Your word is a light upon my path."

The Bible can show us the path where we should go just like the flashlight lighting up my reflector strips. The Bible tells us how our lives can function better.

I find the Bible certainly shows us how to be properly connected to God and it is filled with lots of practical, helpful ideas. It is an excellent guide for living and life just works much better when we follow the guide of the Bible.

The Bible is like the flashlight that shows us how to avoid danger. Living the way the Bible teaches is a lot safer!

I would urge you to read the Bible and then live by what it says. You will be amazed at how practical it can be and how life works so much better when you live it God's way.

Bible
Reference
Psalm 119:
105

D^{og} Training

Those of us who have a hunting dog or have hunted over a dog realize the importance of training. Any dog owner needs to do some obedience training, but a person wishing to train a dog for hunting not only needs to have some form of obedience down, but also needs to train in the area of that dog's specialty. One would work with a pointing dog in a different manner than a retriever. For a pointer you may spend hours using a bird wing with a fishing pole; but with a retriever you would spend a lot of time tossing something into a lake or pond. A different focus would be attempted with a pointing dog than with a flushing dog. In the field, it is obvious which dogs are well trained.

Any trained dog has his bad moments, but untrained dogs are miserable to hunt around. They will bump birds out of range or even catch them. For instance, one day when I was out pheasant hunting and came across two hunters hunting over a brace of pointers. I could see rooster tails sticking out of their game pouches, so they must have been successful. I asked them how they did, and this was their response: "Dogs 2, hunters 0." That day it might have been the weather conditions as the birds were sitting very tight, but normally that would be a very disgusting thing to have your dog break point and catch a bird.

As people, we often get involved in various types of training. Sometimes we get involved in physical

Training

in

godliness

53

training. Our kids are in some sport and there is a lot of physical training for that sport. If we are planning a rugged hunting trip, we need to do a lot of training before we go on that trip. I talked to a person recently who does some aggressive hunts at high altitude and he described how he walks to work (a couple of miles) with a back pack with increasing weights just to get ready for the hunt out west.

The Bible talks about another type of training that we need to be involved in and the results will be quite evident. The Bible says:

"For physical training has some value, but godliness
has value for all things, holding promise for the
present life and the life to come."

The best way to train ourselves in godliness is to learn what God expects as he describes it in the Bible. The Bible is not just a set of dos and don'ts. It tells us who God is, what he is like, and how we can be properly connected to him. It also tells us how to live. I find that living the way the Bible describes makes life work best and it also pleases God.

Let the Bible be your guide for how you live and how you relate to others. Training involves time and exercise. Training in godliness involves time in the Bible and in learning what it says. And it involves exercise, practicing what the Bible says.

Several of us spend many, many hours in training a dog and that training never quits. We constantly reinforce what we taught before. People involved in sports spend many hours in practicing for their sport.

How much time are you spending in training that has

eternal value? Give some thought to how much you are involved in this spiritual training and how much you are practicing it in your life. Train yourself in godliness. Perhaps you give a lot of time to train your dog. You may spend time making sure you are in good physical shape. But how much spiritual or religious training are you involved in?

"For physical training has some value, but godliness has value for all things, holding promise for the present life and the life to come."

Bible
Reference
I Timothy
4:7,8

A Tree by the Riverside

Much of our whitetail hunting in Michigan is on or near farmland; this is especially true in the southern part of the state. Of course, there is more "wild land" further up north.

Each summer we carefully review the crops that are near our hunting ground because we know that they will have an influence on deer patterns in the fall. Cornfields are like timber to whitetails, and carrot fields make excellent feeding grounds. On the other hand a bean field will probably ripen and be harvested early in the season, so it does not offer much attraction, and potato fields are even worse.

Another factor that affects many of the crops is how much moisture we get during the spring, summer, and fall. If there is too much moisture in the spring, that will result in really late harvests. If there is not enough moisture in the summer there may be an early harvest (except in areas where farmers irrigate). Lots of rain in the fall leads to a late harvest time as well. Each of these factors has an influence on the patterns of the deer where we hunt.

Moisture makes a big difference. The Bible talks about how moisture affects a tree. In fact it compares our lives to two kinds of trees. The one life is compared to a stunted shrub in the midst of a barren desert. It is contrasted to a tree that grows by the riverside that not

CK OLD KENT

Old Kent Foundation
One Vandenberg Center
Grand Rapids, Michigan 49503

only looks healthy but also produces an abundance of fruit.

How would you describe your religious/spiritual life? Be honest now. Is your spiritual life more like a stunted shrub in the midst of the desert or like a bean or corn field that lacks moisture, or is your life more like a fruit tree on a river bank which is loaded with good fruit?

The passage in the Bible that draws this contrast says that we have a choice to make that will result in these differences – that choice is TRUST. If we trust in our own selves or rely on human strength or counsel, we will be like the stunted shrub in the desert. On the other hand, if we keep on trusting in God and let our roots grow deep in him, he will produce the new life and then later the fruit in our lives.

Where are you placing your trust? It is easy for us to be so busy in life that we leave no room for God, or almost without thinking, we live by the world's system of values which leaves God out of the picture. It is no wonder that we so often are barren and empty inside. What a difference when we put our trust in God and yield to his leadership in our lives as we invite his Spirit to do in and through us what he wants. Not only do we sense the difference inside us, we actually see God working through us to make a positive impact on people around us.

Tell God you are trusting in him. Surrender control of your life to him daily and see what difference it makes.

Bible
Reference
Jeremiah
17: 1-10

C ampfire

The

Importance

of

Church

Campfires are an everyday experience in the outdoor world. This dates back to years ago when meals were cooked over a fire but moves ahead to the present time when just the sound of the word may bring to mind the pleasant aroma of burning wood or the delicious taste of a marshmallow or a "smore." A fire has warmed many after they have gotten chilled by the cold or after getting wet.

When it comes to fires, we have also learned to be careful. We must be careful where we build them, make sure the conditions are proper for a fire, and carefully put them out. We certainly do not want little children to be unsupervised around fires.

When it comes to fires, what intrigues me the most are the glowing coals. One can watch the changing colors and coals give off an abundance of heat.

Various methods are used to put a fire out. Some are in safe containers and people just let them burn until they are out of fuel. Sometimes there is water nearby and one can douse it with water. But in high country, one of the common methods is to separate the coals. Coals glow brightly and give us much heat when several of them are close together, but when they are separated they lose their heat and eventually the fire goes out.

Separate the coals and the fire goes out!

I think many of us who are outdoor people are quite

independent. We like to function on our own. God and me and a woods or lake or stream are all that I need. Don't tell me about this church stuff!

In my own life I have grown to appreciate and see the need for other warm, glowing coals being close to me! For a time, "Jesus and Me" may have something going, but over the long haul, I need other Christians. I need people who will pray for me, encourage me, challenge me, and hold me accountable. That's where a good church comes into play, and if I can be more specific, a good Bible-believing church which stresses small groups.

You may not want to "spill your guts on the table in front of someone else," as someone once told me about a group he attended; but you will find that praying, caring, supporting, challenging Christians will help to keep your spiritual fire burning. The Bible says:

"And let us consider how we may spur one another on toward love and good deeds. Let us not give up meeting together, as some are in the habit of doing, but let us encourage one another "

Doesn't that sound like warm glowing coals keeping the fire going? It certainly doesn't sound like independent individualism.

Perhaps you have had some disappointing experiences with church or with other people, or perhaps even with other Christians and are trying to "go it alone." On the other hand, I think you sense the need for good, wholesome relationships. The right kind of church is a good place for this to happen. If you are not active in a church, check out what is available in your area. If you know any Christians, ask them where they go and see if you could join them some Sunday. Keep your fire burning.

Bible Reference Hebrews 10:24, 25

Additional Reading Hebrews 3:13

Interesting Protection

I
nteresting
    Protection

God's

Protection

I had one morning to hunt turkeys. It was the last day of the season and this was my last chance at taking a tom. I got out early to an area where I knew they were roosting. I had seen them repeatedly roost in certain trees and then move to the open field at light. I determined to sit in a fence row along the edge. I quietly walked out there. To my surprise, turkeys started flying out of the trees overhead. They had changed their roosting pattern and they were in the trees right above me. After some very noisy escapes, they left the area. I figured my hunting was over for the morning after all the commotion they made leaving.

I waited about 20 minutes and then heard some movement in the grass behind me. I froze and remained as quiet as possible. I watched as first one, then a second, and a third turkey came out of the grass into the field. I strained to see if any beard was showing, but I could not see any. I thought they were jakes, but I could not see any beards.

The turkeys started moving out into the open field. They were almost within range and were circling my way. By this time I could see that they were all three legal birds. I wasn't determind to take a trophy, so any of these would suffice for a good meal.

About that time I heard more noise in the grass. I carefully looked in that direction expecting to see another turkey come out. Surprisingly, four deer came out of the grass about 20 yards from me and walked into the field. One was a nice young buck, and the other three appeared to be does. The buck had a small rack of velvet already starting on his head. But their position posed a problem, because the deer were now between the turkeys and me.

Then something happened that I have never seen before. All four deer starting rounding up the turkeys and chasing them away. Apparently they both wanted to feed in the same area, so the deer rounded them up like a cattle dog and chased them further out into the field. They did this about three times until the turkeys were well out of range, and they came back and continued grazing near me. About that time I saw movement on the other side of the bush next to me and through the branches I could see a huge tom moving out into the field and he was only about 30 yards away! I had to wait until he got far enough out, as I was behind this thick bush, but I got my gun in position and was waiting.

About that time, though, the young buck decided to move and he walked right between the turkey and me. He was curious and tried to figure out what was different about the surroundings, so he kept stretching and sniffing but moved more and more in between the turkey and me. The deer was only about 10 yards from me and the turkey was probably about 25 yards away but directly behind this buck. Well, I never did get a shot. The deer, without knowing it, were protecting the turkeys.

This fall, my son, had a reversal of that experience. One morning, shortly after he got into his stand a whole flock of turkeys moved under his tree. At first he thought deer were approaching with all the noise they made in the leaves, but it didn't take long before a rather large flock starting eating under his tree. A little while later he saw two deer approaching, so he got ready for a shot. To his amazement, the turkeys formed a protective guard and would not allow the deer to come any further. They formed a circle and would not let the deer in. The deer began to stomp and snort, and eventually walked away and never came in. A little while later, they tried again, coming in from a different angle, but with the same result. The turkeys quickly moved into a circle and did not let the deer advance.

I was trying to shoot a turkey and the deer protected them. My son was trying to harvest a deer and the turkeys protected the deer.

As I reflect on these experiences, I am reminded of God's protection. How many times we have had his protective guard. I still don't know how I made it around the curve in the mountains in Colorado. A vehicle was approaching me out of control. There was only room for one vehicle on the road at that curve but somehow we both made it around that curve. I was on the outside edge. Or take another situation. I recall a time when my son was looking into an abandoned mine when the ground started to give way and he started to slide in. It was almost miraculous that a friend could just reach out in time and grab him. I think of the times traveling at night, when I must have dozed off, but woke up before the car went off the edge of the road. I could go on and list many more times when it was obvious that I had some special protection.

The Bible talks about God's protection in many places. One of the most remarkable is in the Psalms. There it talks about how intimately God knows us – he knows our thoughts, he knows when we sit down and when we stand. He even knows the words we are going to say before we say them. When I think about his knowledge, my first reaction is to be scared if God knows everything about me. But the psalmist goes on to tell us that even though God knows everything about us, he still loves us and cares for us and wants to protect us. It is like he goes ahead to make the way safe and sets up a protective guard behind us so we won't be blind sided.

There are times when God allows difficulties and then works through them to make our lives better, but many times God sends his angels to protect us.

Today reflect on your life and how often you have experienced that protection, and then thank God for his protective guard around your life.

Additional
Reading
Psalm 139:
1-12

A Gentle Breeze or a Strong Wind

The Holy Spirit is like a gentle breeze on a hot day

Early season hunting can be very uncomfortable on warm days. Even though we try to dress appropriately for what game we are pursuing, often our dress seems to be better suited for cooler conditions. Where can you find good camo for a hot day? Even long sleeve shirts are uncomfortably warm, but I don't feel like using face paint over my arms and a long sleeved shirt can help in warding off those nasty mosquitoes.

How refreshing it is on a hot day to feel a gentle breeze! Hot conditions are much more bearable when there is a gentle wind. I remember dove hunting in Illinois. We hunted early September in the south central part of the state and it was very hot. On opening day the season began at noon. I was hunting a public area with one of my boys. We had hunted this area before, so we arrived about 9:30am to get a good spot and to get set up. Then we waited for noon to come. As we waited along the edge of a sunflower field, it felt so refreshing to have a light wind blowing.

The Bible talks about the wind. It describes how the Holy Spirit functions as being like a wind. God touches and affects our lives through the wind of his Spirit. I find that this is often like a gentle, refreshing breeze. When I am discouraged from the stress of the day, God lets the gentle breeze of his Spirit bring encouragement to my life. It might be a song that lifts my spirits or an encouraging word from a friend or perhaps a thought from the Bible that readjusts my focus. As refreshing as a gentle breeze is on a hot day, so refreshing is God's Spirit touching my inner life.

Sometimes I need a stronger wind to blow in my life. I am often amazed at how powerful wind can be. Trees can be uprooted and other items repositioned with very strong winds. We deer hunt in an area where a severe windstorm came though a couple of years ago. Huge oaks and maples were uprooted. Wind can be so powerful that it can uproot a hardwood tree. Sometimes I get so stuck in bad patterns, or my relationship with God needs some serious readjustment, that it takes a stronger wind of the Spirit to get me back on track. Experiencing this change may not be as pleasant as a gentle breeze on a hot day, but it is very helpful in the long run.

Where are you today? Do you need a gently encouraging, refreshing breeze of the Spirit or do you need a stronger wind to get you back on course or to reposition your life? Invite God's Spirit to be at work in your life.

The Holy Spirit is sometimes like a strong wind that readjusts our lives

Additional Reading
Acts 2:1-13;
John 16:5-15;
Ephesians 3:20,21

Broken Equipment

Broken

Hearts

Broken equipment, who hasn't had that problem? Last fall we went to Iowa to hunt pheasants with some of my friends. One of my friends had purchased a new gun a short time before, a very reliable model. He had done some shooting before the trip, and had some problems with his new gun, so he returned it to be fixed. After getting it fixed, he shot it several times and it seemed to be working well. But when we were in Iowa, his gun did not work properly again. Something must have been broken.

Guns don't break very often, but what about archery equipment? We tend to have more failures here.
Knocks break or come off. Arrows get bent or broken.
Perhaps we have even had a bow string break on us. If we expand our circles, and think about our hunting vehicles, our nice trucks; think about how many times have we taken them in for repair because something was broken.

We get used to things that are broken, but one thing seems to creep up on us that we don't expect is when we are broken.

Broken hearted – broken spirit. That's no fun, but so many of us have been there! I have and you probably have been there also. I don't want to dwell on a depressing theme, but only use it to point out something about God and how He works. The Psalmist in the

Bible talks so honestly about being broken. He says this:

"I have become like broken pottery."

Like a broken glass or a broken vase, parts and pieces lying all around. The Psalmist says, 'I am there.' That describes my life. I have become broken! Later the same Psalmist describes it this way:

"let the bones, which you have crushed, rejoice."

I don't think the Psalmist was just talking about broken bones. He was using that illustration to describe how he felt. He felt broken.

There is something good about being broken. I don't mean that this is an enjoyable experience. Personally I remember one night when I felt so broken. It happened at deer camp. I was bowhunting with some friends. I received a phone call which left me shattered inside. But can you show this in front of rough and tough outdoor bow hunters? I tried to hide it. But that night as I was out hunting, I was weeping so much that I could not even get a shot off.

I had nine deer within shooting range, including two decent bucks, but I was such a broken mess, that I couldn't even get my bow up for a shot. No – that wasn't fun! I did not enjoy that time. I felt hurt, scared, depressed; I felt like a failure. But something about being broken gets God's attention.

Durinng the next days when I felt so broken, I felt so close to God. I sensed his presence; I experienced his love. He didn't come and wave a magic wand and fix everything, but he was there close to me, when I felt so alone and hurt. The Bible says that God will not ignore a broken spirit.

He will not put down a broken and contrite heart. It gives him something pliable to work with. God knows that at these moments we are most dependent upon Him. The Psalmist later puts it this way:

"He heals the brokenhearted and binds up their wounds."

Not a quick fix, but gradual, gentle, soothing, loving care. Even more than that, God can use us in his plan to do something better when we are broken. Think of a glass of water. If it was being filled, it could overflow when it got full. But if that same glass had a large crack in it and we proceeded to pour water into it, the water would leak out.

I have found God works this way. We are just a container, an "earthen vessel," but God lives inside us and his power can work through us. He can certainly fill us to overflowing. But more often He uses us when we are broken. We become more sensitive to others. We can relate to them better.

Bible Reference Psalm 31:12; 51:8, 147:3

Additional Reading Psalm 38:8; Isaiah 57:15

God's love and grace can flow through the broken cracks in our lives and influence others in a positive way. Do you have broken equipment, broken hearts? Let God heal you. And let God's love and grace flow through the breaks and cracks in your life.

C hickadee -- A Special Reminder

I remember a time as a young person when I had a chickadee eat out of my hand. It took persistence and many attempts but finally one of these beautiful little birds felt safe enough to eat out of my hand. That seemed like quite an accomplishment to me at the time.

Now it seems like chickadees can be found almost anywhere in these northern woods. Sitting in a deer blind in the thickest part of the forest, and suddenly a group of chickadees appear with their cheerful sound. Wading back into the thickest swamp where nothing else seems to be moving, except hopefully a nice buck before evening falls, when suddenly there is the whistling and the familiar call of the chickadee. Sitting still in a tree stand or a blind and chickadees come so close they may even sit on your gun barrel or on a branch right next to you.

For me the chickadee has become a reminder of God's presence. We can be in the darkest situation in life and God is still there. We can face the most challenging obstacle and God will be there. We can be relaxing and enjoying the beauty around us, and God will be there. The Psalmist knew this well. He says,

"O Lord, you have searched me and you know me. You know when I sit and when I rise; you perceive my thoughts from afar. You discern my going out and my lying down. You are familiar with all my

A Reminder of God's Presence

ways. Before a word is on my tongue you know it completely, O Lord"

How wonderful to think that God is so close to us he can know what is going on in our lives. It is amazing to comprehend that God knows everything about us! It's scary to realize that he even knows what we are thinking. But even more remarkable is what the Psalmist goes on to say. He tells us that even though God is close enough to know everything about us and even though he can see right inside us, he is there to love and protect us!

When Jesus was getting ready to leave this world he told his followers to focus on his work of making disciples of all kinds of people everywhere, but then he left a beautiful promise:

"And surely I am with you always, to the very end of the age."

Jesus also promised to send his spirit who would not only be near us but literally come to live inside us when we become Christians.

Bible
Reference
Psalm
139:1,2
Mathew
28:20

Additional
Reading
Psalm 139;
Mathew
28:18-20

When you see a chickadee in the darkness of the forest or the dampness of the swamp; when you find a group of these cheerful little birds surrounding you; then remember that God is closer than even a chickadee. He knows and understands what is going on in our lives and he wants to protect and help us.

Sometimes we may feel like we are running away from God, but there is no place we can go to escape his presence. We don't have to be afraid of him, because even though he knows what we are like and what we are going through, he is there to help us.

Hunting the Rut

Most of us who hunt deer know that bucks make stupid mistakes during the rut. This is the time of the year they are most vulnerable. For the past few years, I have scheduled some vacation time for bowhunting when we anticipated a peak rut time. Studies have been done to try to determine when the peak rut time will be or when we will hit the highest point of buck activity relating to the rut. Some believe moon phases affect the rut; while other people conclude that other conditions bring on the rut.

Some things we know: There is a time when a buck stakes out his territory and actively defends it. Each buck develops a rub line. Scrapes are made and some are revisited again and again. Eventually the time will come when a buck starts to actively follow does. Smaller bucks seems to have the least amount of caution, that is why most people shoot a smaller buck. The older bucks are generally more wary.

But even older bucks make a few crazy mistakes. A hunter can see a nice big buck following a doe right in the middle of the day. Many hunters have watched a nice buck walk right out into the open and make himself vulnerable to the hunter. There may be only a few wise old monster bucks around that are completely nocturnal.

With sex on his mind, the buck makes some pretty

stupid mistakes. Often our lives are a lot like the rut. Look at how many crazy, stupid, no-brainer mistakes we make because some desire or drive gets the best of us

Sex. How many messed up situations have resulted by letting a sexual desire get out of control? How many relationships broke apart and new ones didn't really get established because of uncontrolled passion?

Money and Spending. How many of us haven't made stupid mistakes buying things we didn't need, buying something that cost more than we could afford just because we wanted it, because some desire for it exceeded making sense?

Substance abuse. How many haven't done stupid things when they were out of control under the influence of some other substance?

We all have made some bad choices. We have made stupid decisions, no brainers, like our brain went to sleep and our passions took over. We have made wrong choices and some of us suffer some severe consequences of those decisions, broken relationships, guilt, same, perhaps even some physical problems or symptoms.

What can we conclude? With God there is forgiveness even when we mess up. The Bible says:

"Though your sins are like scarlet, they shall be as white as snow."

Scarlet was the brightest color in Bible days. Though our sins are as obvious and out in the open as hunter orange, God says he can make us clean and fresh as new fallen snow. The Bible goes on to say:

> "Though they are red as crimson, they shall be as
> wool."

Crimson was a bright deep red made from a permanent dye. In Old Testament times they didn't have a way to remove a permanent dye. God is saying even though we seem to have a permanently engrained habit or addiction to sin, God can make us new again, just like a raw piece of wool.

No brainers, rut-induced mistakes, passions over rational thinking, let God forgive and give you a new, clean, fresh heart and life.

Bible
Reference
Isaiah 1:18

Additional
Reading
II Timothy
2:22;
I Corinthians
10:13

Playing Dead

Be under

the

influence

of the

Holy Spirit

not

alcohol

My youngest two sons each have their own Brittanys, Prince and Shadow. We have a kennel area in our backyard where they stay during the day, and in the evening we have a kennel area in the basement where they can stay at night. We have an automatic feeder that keeps them supplied with food, as they need it.

We began to notice each morning that something had been getting into the automatic feeder. The cover was tipped up almost every morning when we brought the dogs out.

We kept the gate closed at night, so we knew another dog couldn't get it. I kept putting heavier and heavier objects on the cover, but they would still be tipped off in the morning. We thought that either a coon or a possum must be getting into their food at night.

One night my son came home fairly late and went out to take the dogs in. He noticed that an opossum was lying in the cage. It looked dead, just lying there still. He thought the dogs might have killed it or it might have just been "playing dead."

He called the dogs. Prince came to him, but Shadow decided to make an interesting retrieve. Shadow went over to the opossum and picked it up and brought it to my son and dropped it at his feet. A beautiful retrieve! Suddenly the opossum woke up right at my son's feet. He wasn't dead; he just looked that way.

I have been told that opossums don't "play dead." When in a frightening situation there is some change that happens which shuts down their system so they look dead (another of God's fascinating designs!).

When I reflect on this opossum "playing dead" it reminds me of something similar that a lot of people have happen to them without even realizing it. That is what happens with the over use of alcohol or other drugs. What most people don't realize is that alcohol causes us to "play dead." Or to put it differently, alcohol shuts down our system – our brain - so it doesn't function properly. It doesn't take much, perhaps only two beers or something stronger and part of our brain goes to sleep. We do not notice it and don't realize that our behavior changes. But just ask others around you, a friend or spouse or child, and they will tell you how your lifestyle changes.

The Bible tells us not to be controlled by alcohol or drugs but instead to be under the influence of the Holy Spirit. Being under the power of the Holy Spirit results in having a deeper internal peace and calmness; a joy that radiates from our being, improved relationships, and a lifestyle that is very appealing. On the other hand look at all the damage and problems alcohol use/abuse can bring – broken and destroyed relationships, fear and concern about activities you were involved in, and a lifestyle that keeps bringing more and more problems.

Are you going to "play dead?" Are you going to allow alcohol to put your brain to sleep?
Instead let God's Spirit fill you, control you, lead you and you will be amazed at how much better life goes!

Bible Reference
Ephesians
5:15-20

75

Getting Even

I was out hunting with some friends. It was shortly after we moved to Michigan. They invited me along to go woodcock and grouse hunting and I could take my Brittany along. We had lived in Illinois and Dusty had never hunted anything other than pheasants and quail, so I wondered how it would work out to hunt woodcock. He was used to hunting farmland with fencerows and had never hunted in a swamp and woods before.

We drove up to this hunting area with my friends. We got out of the car and got ready to hunt. When we were set, I took my dog out. As we moved into the woods I could see that Dusty was pretty excited about hunting, but he did not seem to catch on to woodcock hunting. If the woodcock were in, he was blowing right by them; but the reports said that the migration had begun and this was an ideal spot.

After the initial rush, my dog tired out a little and slowed down; at that point he suddenly starting pointing woodcock and grouse. In fact, he had several points in a row. The first bird escaped our ammunition, but we managed to put down the second and a couple after that.

I wondered if Dusty would retrieve a woodcock. He was much stronger on point and somewhat weak on retrieving, but he always found the bird for me. If he didn't retrieve it, he would simply lock on point over it until I got there. I had heard that some dogs don't like to retrieve woodcocks because of their scent.

When we shot one I carefully watched where it landed and sent my dog after it. He went right to the woodcock that was down, took one sniff, and walked away and started hunting. We picked up that bird and decided that we needed to watch where they fell, because it didn't seem like my dog was going to retrieve these new flying creatures, but at least he was pointing them now.

I could tell Dusty was really getting tired. It was early in the season and it was a very hot day, so after a few hours he was really getting weary. By this time, though, we had basically completed this hunt. We were planning to eat lunch and then go to a different spot and bowhunt in the evening.

Getting

Even

I had my dog heeling right next to me as we walked out of the woods. Suddenly Dusty locked on point — I mean locked on point. His head was cocked, his foot was up, and there he stood as firm as could be. I looked. No bird; just some leaves, not even brush for a bird to hide under.

By this time we were joking around and having a good time and the two guys with me were starting to make fun of my dog. They thought that he was pointing some old scent of a bird that had been there and left.

I kicked the leaves and nothing flew, so I decided to call my dog off, or more literally I pulled him off point and started toward the car. He took about two steps and went right back there and locked on point. Now this was getting a little embarrassing. There was no bird there, just a few leaves. I had kicked the leaves and nothing had come out.

I went back and rustled the leaves again when suddenly to my amazement a woodcock flew up from under his nose right out of those leaves I had kicked a few times. Well we were talking and joking around so much not one of us even got a gun up and we watched the bird sail away without a shot taken.

I looked at Dusty and he looked me straight in the eye; then he looked at my friend and then the other friend. I do not think dogs can reason like we do, but that look seemed to say: "I did all this for you and now you don't even shoot!"

Now it was time to leave, so he was on heel again and we were walking out of the woods. We went about six feet and he locked up on point again. This time we were more serious about the situation. We got our guns ready and moved over his point. We flushed the bird, shot, and dropped it. It fell in some really long grass.

One of my friends said; "I'll go over there and get my camera ready maybe Dusty will go on point when he gets near the bird." The other friend who had shot the woodcock went to look for his bird. I sent Dusty in to look although I didn't expect much after watching him ignore woodcock before.

All of a sudden I heard my friends start to laugh and they laughed and laughed! I couldn't figure out what they were laughing about. Finally they came out of the long grass, but were not carrying the bird, and still were laughing.

One of them came up and said, "Your dog urinated on my bird!" When they found the bird, they called Dusty. He came up to the bird like he was going to pick it up, but then proceeded to stand above it and urinated all over it. It was almost like he was getting even. "I did all that and you didn't shoot. I'll get even with you guys!" Even if dogs cannot reason like us, it sure appeared like he was getting even.

Getting even. How often we are prone to get even with someone, from the time we are kids up until we are adults? Someone does something to us that is not nice, we are going to return the "favor." Someone does us in, he better look out.

Notice how often that happens in marriages, for those of us who are married. One does something, the spouse does something else to get even!

The Bible speaks about this subject. It is almost like Jesus knew that we would have a problem in this area. Listen to what is says

"Do not repay any one evil for evil. Be careful to do what is right in the eyes of everyone. If it is possible, as far as it depends upon you, live at peace with everyone. Do not take revenge my friends, but leave room for God's wrath, for it is written; 'It is mine to avenge; I will repay' says the Lord."

God says don't repay evil for evil; don't get even. God says he will take care of the matter. Instead, as much as we are able, we must live peaceably with all. This doesn't mean that all will treat us this way, but we must initiate the action; we must treat others in a way that will bring peace.

Perhaps someone has really hurt you. Perhaps your marriage broke down or is breaking down right now.

Look at how eager you are to repay evil for evil. Look at how much you desire to get even.

Instead, the Bible says live differently. Don't repay evil for evil. Don't get even. Let God handle the matter. Instead – we must work at restoring relationships! This is not saying we put up with everything; that we just become rugs and let people walk all over us. This is not saying that we let abuse happen, but on the other hand, it means we treat others with kindness and respect. We do what we can to build up and restore relationships instead of tearing them down and blowing them apart.

Will you live life God's way with his help?

Bible
Reference
Romans
12:17-19

Bufflehead Display

One thing I like about spring and fall is to watch the migrating birds. I especially enjoy seeing waterfowl. We see many different types of birds than what we see during the summer.

One particular evening I was by a lake and it was enjoyable trying to identify the different species of ducks that stopped by on their trip back to the north country. I saw a variety of mergansers, golden eyes, buffleheads, and some others that were too far away to get a good identification.

As I was watching four Buffleheads moved in close to where I was – two males and two females. It was fascinating to watch the awesome display these two males were making for the females. They would fly a short distance and then have a fancy slide right up to one of the females. They would act as if they would be taking off, but then stay right there and make a fascinating display beating their wings right in front of each female. One female moved away from the group and one of the males joined her and continued to put on show in front of her. She must have been pleased because they disappeared together under the water. This amazing scene was repeated a few times. Eventually she had enough and flew away to the other side of the lake.

While all this was going on, the other male was trying hard to impress the other female and seemed to be doing a good job of it. Then I noticed the first male tried to cut in on his territory. This first male put on an even more splendid presentation in front of this other female. At first she didn't seem to be interested in him, she stayed close to the other male, but eventually he won her over and the other male was left out and flew away.

As I thought about what happened, it reminded me of many conversations I have had with people and other situations I have observed. It seems common in our world where a man isn't satisfied with only one woman, but moves on to the next. Or a woman may be connected to one man and then another man seems more attractive. It seems so appealing. Feelings are so strong (or at least become that way). The new person seems to have so much more to offer. But if one moves on to satisfy those feelings, destruction and damage lies ahead.

Listen to some words from the Bible on this subject when it says that he saw a person:

> "who lacked judgment; he was going down the street near her corner, walking alone in the direction of her house, at twilight, as the day was fading, as the dark of night set in   "

Then we read a little later:

> The woman talking: "I came out to meet you. I looked for you and found you   come let's drink deep of love till morning, let's enjoy ourselves with love! My husband is not home; he has gone on a long journey."

But then notice the conclusion a little later:

"All at once he followed her like an ox going to the slaughter, like a deer stepping into a noose til an arrow pierces his liver. Like a bird darting into a snare, little knowing it will cost him his life."

Some of you have been there. You know what I'm talking about. You have experienced the destruction and damage. You have seen kids get hurt and saw how life gets complicated. Sometimes even physical diseases complicate these activities.

Doesn't God's way make more sense? After all He designed marriage and it works best when we do it his way. He expects us to be faithful to our spouse.

"You shall not commit adultery." (you shall not get sexually involved with someone other than your spouse).

He makes his point and then gives us the power to live that way. Plus there is nothing wrong with getting professional help if our relationship is stressed out. We don't hesitate to take a vehicle in to a professional to get something fixed when it is not working properly. Why will we do this for metal and plastic and fail to maintain or "fix" a relationship which is far more precious?

Keep on staying faithful to your spouse with God's help.

If you have messed up and gotten involved in an improper relationship, God is willing to forgive and can help you rebuild your life. But you will still have to deal with some of the consequences of your past actions.

God doesn't wave some magical wand over past behavior to erase the results. He is willing to pardon where we are guilty, and he is offering to heal and help rebuild our lives. Will you let him? Will you turn to him and ask for his help and then continue to follow his leading in the future?

With God's help, let's live the way he wants us to, and we will find that life works best that way.

Bible Reference Proverbs 7:8, 9, 15, 18, 19 Exodus 20:14

Bible Reference Proverbs 7; Exodus 20

S cent

It is always amazing to watch one of our Brittanies smell birds and then point them. If you watch the dogs, you can notice when they get "birdy." Their little tails start moving fast; you can see they are excited, and then they go on point. What could smell so good or so bad that they could notice it?

It is also interesting to watch a deer respond to scent. I was out turkey hunting and was not worried about my scent, but paid extra special attention to avoiding movement. As I was watching a couple of turkeys some distance away, a big buck with nice velvet starting coming my way. He looked very relaxed and was very beautiful. But I knew that he was headed down wind of me and I wondered how he would react when he came across my scent. He looked like an older buck, so he must have survived the previous hunting seasons. As this buck continued walking and moved down wind of where I was sitting, he suddenly became very alert, took one good sniff, and quickly bounded away.

Do I smell that bad? How did he notice my scent? Certainly animals have a keener sense of smell than humans. We get a strong unpleasant odor from a skunk; and some other things smell really good to us, like certain flowers or good food or the right kind of perfume.

The Bible talks about "body odor." It says that we are the aroma of Christ.

We must give off a good aroma to attract others to a relationship with Jesus Christ

85

"We are to God the aroma of Christ among those who are being saved and among those who are perishing. To the one we are the smell of death. To the other the fragrance of life."

If we are Christians, our lives let off an aroma. To some it is not a pleasant odor, but a deathly odor. Those who reject Christianity do not like to be around us. But for others it is different. They smell a pleasant aroma. They like what they smell. They want to experience this change in life also. What we have is attractive to them. They are led into a relationship with God through what they sense in our lives.

How about you? Are you still trying to detect the aroma? Are you still exploring Christianity? You like a lot of what you see. You are attracted to it. You can sense it is real in the lives of some people you know.

Or are you a Christian? Are you connected closely enough to Christ that you are giving off a very pleasant aroma which attracts others to Christ?

Additional
Reading
II
Corinthians
2:12-18

86

Personal Property

I don't know what it is like in your state, but in Michigan we have to sign our hunting license as soon as we receive it. In fact, at most sporting goods stores that sell them, they hand you your new license and ask you to sign it right on the spot.

We often put our names on things that belong to us. We engrave our names on our treestands. We have had some stolen and we hope that this discourages that practice (plus a piece of logging chain and a good padlock).

Last year I was visiting with one of the neighbors of our hunting land. We were talking about hunting and he asked me if we ever watched deer during the summer. I said that we usually do not, except for some legal shining with the kids. He then asked if we kept treestands up all year. I asked what he meant. He said that he found some stands on the piece of land that we lease and one had a certain name on it. He wondered if I knew that person. The name he mentioned was my brother–in–law who leases that piece with me. A few days later I told this to my brother–in–law. He said that his name was inscribed on the topside of his treestand.

The only way this person would know the name would mean that he had climbed the tree and was sitting up in his treestand. Now I won't comment on the totally

God

is

personally

watching

over

us

illegal activity of this neighbor. In Michigan you are not allowed to step on another person's property without permission. Besides this we had many "no trespassing" signs on that land in very visible locations.

When it comes to our names being placed on what we own, we need to remember that God has a process of putting his name on us. In the Bible, God says:

"See, I have engraved you on the palm of my hands."

God's ownership is obvious. We belong to him. But it is even more personal than that. God writing us on the palm of his hand is like a very personal reminder. Occasionally I use my hand for writing a note or a number that I need to remember. It is there in front of me whenever I open my hand. This verse is not only showing that we belong to God but it is letting us know that God personally watches over us and thinks about us. We have his personal attention.

If you realize that you belong to God, are there any adjustments needed in the way you are living? If you are facing any challenges, realize you are on God's mind because he has written your name on the palm of his hand.

Bible
Reference
Isaiah 49:16

Swamper a New Friend at Hunting Camp

Swamper. I have never seen a dog that is so lovable. But let me tell you a little about this dog. Swamper is not a normal dog. She is not a pup that grew up in the security of her master.

We don't know anything about her earliest life, but one-day Swamper was discovered. Friends of ours who lived next to our hunting cottage were driving down the road and went by a swamp near a wooded area.

As they were going down the road they noticed something that looked rather strange out on a log in the swamp. They stopped the car to get a better look. Here was this fuzz ball of a puppy stranded on a log out in this swamp! She looked so cold and was shivering and was crying for their attention.

We do not know how the dog arrived there. We are not sure if it got lost or if perhaps someone just dropped it off and left it. It was a long way from any home, and those houses that were closest, didn't have this kind of dog, so it is unlikely that it wandered away.

We suspect someone dropped it off, but it looked like an expensive dog, so we wondered why someone wouldn't have tried to sell it if they didn't want it. Maybe it just fell out of a pickup?

We don't know where it came from or even how it got out in that swamp. That swamp was a pretty yucky

He

who is

forgiven

much

loves

much

mess; stinky water all around; and here is a pup out on a slanted tree that rises just above the water.

My friend tried to get some branches to make a way out to this dog, but the water was too deep. And the next thing he knew, this little fuzz ball came swimming through the murky water to them and ran up to them and wanted to be held. They took this stinky, sloppy, little dog home and cleaned it up.

Swamper is the most lovable little pup you have ever seen. All pups seem to be cute; it's just that they grow up into dogs that need lots of attention and care. But Swamper was especially friendly.

They tried to find the owner; spreading the word around if anyone was looking for this cute little pup, but no one claimed it. When no one responded, they thought at first that they would give it to someone; but it did not take long before they fell in love with this little pup themselves.

Even as this little puppy grew up, it still was such a lovable dog. I have never seen a dog that craves love and acceptance like this one, even now — a couple of years later. I can be quite a distance from this dog and when she discovers that I'm there, she comes running to me as fast as she can.

When I am out in our yard, she will come and stand with her feet up against the fence with pleading eyes; one can almost put words into her look, "Won't you please come over and pet me?" This dog reminds me of something Jesus says in the Bible. He says that the one who has been forgiven little, loves little; but the one who has been forgiven much, loves much.

Swamper was out in this disgusting, horrible, smelly

swamp, in danger, scared and lonely, and then was rescued. Sometimes our lives get out of control and we end up in a stinky horrible disgusting swamp. Not literally, but spiritually. We become confused, sad, and lonely. We feel sad and upset. We get down on ourselves and see the bleakness of our situation, and our feelings inside torment us!

We start thinking that God could never accept us based on how awful some of our behavior has been. But a neat thing about Jesus is that He associated with sinners. He lets them know they are loved. He shows them that God can accept them. He leads them to forgiveness.

Can you hear the Pharisees (religious leaders in Jesus' day) talk?

"Jesus, don't you know that this lady is a sinner? This is an immoral woman. She is a public disgrace. You will become ceremonially unclean!"

But Jesus didn't mind the comments; he just loved her into a relationship with his Father.

Today, wherever you are in life, realize that God loves you! God is willing to rescue you from the swamp you are in. God will welcome you back from the hurt, the pain, the fear, and the confusion in your life. God is willing to forgive your guilt and relieve your shame. And as you begin to experience the amazing love of God; you will want to please God more than anything else.

Little Swamper just begs for love and attention; but on the other hand that little dog will do almost anything to please someone. Do you still crave God's love and acceptance? Are you willing to do anything to please him?

Additional Reading Luke 7:36-50

91

Evergreen Trees

Everlasting

Life

I love fall. Not only does that bring the hunting season around, but also the marvelous changing color of the trees. Here in Michigan we are spoiled with the variety colors. I have lived in Colorado and have greatly enjoyed the yellow of the aspen, but nothing quite compares to the bright reds, oranges, and yellows of the hardwoods in a state like this. But, one thing stands out in the midst of bright yellows or reds and oranges, it is the green of the evergreen trees. The dark green shows off in the midst of all the bright colors and it continues to stay green after all the rest have shed their leaves.

Once while deer hunting we saw a deer go into a small grove of pine trees. Someone had wounded this deer, and we decided to try to harvest it. We set up a miniature drive, because the group of evergreens was so small we didn't need many people to cover it. We walked along and through this small group of trees, but no one saw the deer come out. We decided to go back through it again, just in case we had missed it. Again, no one saw the deer. We decided to move on figuring that somehow it had eluded us.

The next morning I returned to that group of pines. There was snow on the ground and I wanted to check to see if that deer was still in there. To my amazement, I found where the deer had been. It had stayed tightly under one tree. We had walked within a few feet of it, and it had not moved out from its cover! It was obvious that it had been there for some time, as there were many droppings under that tree, but before morning came it scampered away. I could tell because we had some light snow toward morning, and the deer tracks went out through that snow. This small group of evergreens provided safety for one deer.

As fall progresses, it gets easier and easier to find one of my favorite treestands. Right at the entrance to the back part of the woods where it is located, is a large pine tree. In early October, when the leaves are still on the other trees, it is not easy to spot this huge pine. But once the trees have shed their leaves, that pine tree is so obvious.

Evergreens. Let them serve as a reminder to us of what the Bible calls eternal or everlasting life.

"For God so loved the world that he gave his one and only son, that whoever believes in him shall not perish but have eternal life."

The Bible teaches that life does not end when we die, but we will live forever. Either we will face an eternal reward which is miserable, called Hell, because we have rejected Jesus Christ, or we will live in a wonderful place called Heaven with God and will live there forever. Our minds cannot comprehend what this will be like, but God tells us that it will be so. If we believe in Jesus, we will have everlasting life. That new and better and more satisfying life starts already now, but it will continue forever even after we die.

We can experience forgiveness of sins, new meaning in life, joy and purpose for living, better relationships, and then a wonderful future in heaven.

As you look around at the various trees and notice the dark green of the evergreens, take some time to evaluate where your life is headed. Have you accepted God's gift of eternal life through faith in Jesus Christ? If not, why not settle that right now?

If you wish to learn more about how to be right with God or if you have found a new relationship with God, please contact me.

Maury De Young
610-52nd St SE
Kentwood, MI 49548
616-534-0085
mdeyoung@kcrc.org

If you wish to learn more about
Kelloggsville Church Sportsperson's Club
www.kcrc.org/sportspersonsclub or email us at spc@kcrc.org